EARTH'S CYCLES IN ACTION

THE CARBON CYCLE

By Diane Dakers

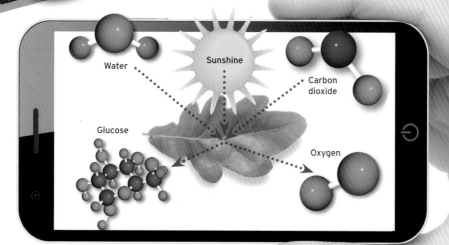

Water
Sunshine
Carbon dioxide
Glucose
Oxygen

CRABTREE
Publishing Company
www.crabtreebooks.com

Crabtree Publishing Company
www.crabtreebooks.com

Author: Diane Dakers
Publishing plan research and development:
Reagan Miller
Project coordinator: Mark Sachner,
Water Buffalo Books
Editors: Mark Sachner, Shirley Duke
Proofreader: Wendy Scavuzzo
Editorial director: Kathy Middleton
Photo researcher: Ruth Owen
Designer: Westgraphix/Tammy West
Contributing writer and indexer: Suzy Gazlay
Production coordinator and prepress technician:
Margaret Amy Salter
Print coordinator: Katherine Berti
Science, reading, and curriculum consultant:
Suzy Gazlay, M.A.; Recipient, Presidential Award
for Excellence in Science Teaching

Written, developed, and produced by
Water Buffalo Books

Photographs and reproductions:
Front Cover: Thinkstock: Nivellen77 (background);
Elenarts (Tyrannosaurus dinosaurs)

Interior: Suzy Gazlay: pp. 42 (center, lower right),
43 (upper left, upper right, center, lower left). **Ruby
Tuesday Books Ltd:** pp. 31, 38 (top). **Science Photo
Library:** pp. 14, 23 (bottom), 39, 40. **Shutterstock:** pp. 1,
3, 4, 5, 6, 7, 8 (top), 9, 10, 11, 12, 13, 15, 16, 17, 18, 19, 20,
21, 22, 23 (top), 24, 25, 27, 28 (center), 28 (right), 29, 30,
32, 33, 34, 35, 36, 37, 45, 42 (background, upper right), 43
(background, lower right), 46, 48. **Shutterstock:** wdeon:
p. 8; N.F. Photography: p. 38 (bottom). **Prof. Gordon T.
Taylor, Stony Brook University:** p. 26, 28 (left).

Library and Archives Canada Cataloguing in Publication

Dakers, Diane, author
        The carbon cycle / Diane Dakers.

(Earth's cycles in action)
Includes index.
Issued in print and electronic formats.
ISBN 978-0-7787-0672-4 (bound).--
ISBN 978-0-7787-0621-2 (pbk.).--
ISBN 978-1-4271-7625-7 (pdf).--ISBN 978-1-4271-7621-9 (html)

        1. Carbon cycle (Biogeochemistry)--Juvenile literature.
I. Title.

QH344.D35 2014   j577'.144   C2014-903931-X
                                                                        C2014-903932-8

Library of Congress Cataloging-in-Publication Data

Dakers, Diane, author.
        The carbon cycle / Diane Dakers.
                pages cm. -- (Earth's cycles in action)
        Includes index.
        ISBN 978-0-7787-0672-4 (reinforced library binding) --
        ISBN 978-0-7787-0621-2 (pbk.) --
        ISBN 978-1-4271-7625-7 (electronic pdf) --
        ISBN 978-1-4271-7621-9 (electronic html)
        1. Carbon cycle (Biogeochemistry)--Juvenile literature. I. Title.

QH344.D37 2015
577.144--dc23

                                        2014032598

Crabtree Publishing Company
www.crabtreebooks.com   1-800-387-7650

Printed in Canada/102014/EF20140925

**Published
in Canada
Crabtree Publishing**
616 Welland Ave.
St. Catharines, Ontario
L2M 5V6

**Published in
the United States
Crabtree Publishing**
PMB 59051
350 Fifth Ave., 59th Floor
New York, NY 10118

**Published in the
United Kingdom
Crabtree Publishing**
Maritime House
Basin Road North, Hove
BN41 1WR

**Published
in Australia
Crabtree Publishing**
3 Charles Street
Coburg North
VIC, 3058

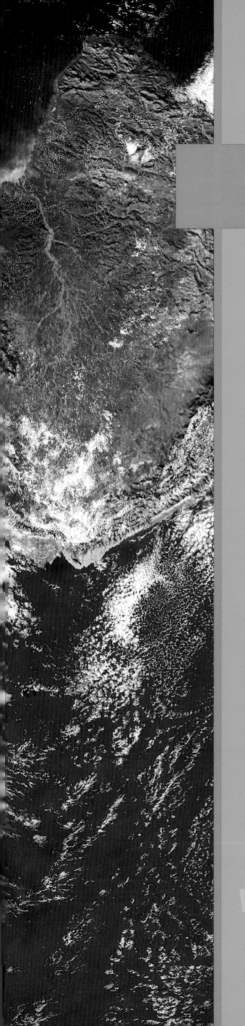

Contents

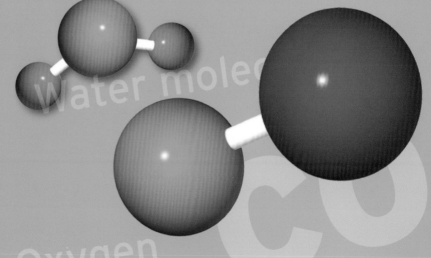

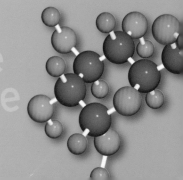

CHAPTER 1

Why Care About Carbon?

Every living thing—plant and animal—contains carbon. In fact, about 18 percent of your body is carbon. That means, if you weigh 100 pounds (45 kilograms), you contain 18 pounds (8 kg) of carbon. That's about the weight of a car tire or sledgehammer!

Tiny Building Blocks

Everything in the world is made up of **atoms** and **molecules**. Atoms and molecules are submicroscopic. This means they are so small that they cannot be seen with an ordinary microscope. Atoms are individual building blocks, and molecules are combinations of those building blocks.

The **periodic table** lists 118 known chemical **elements** and the atoms that make them.

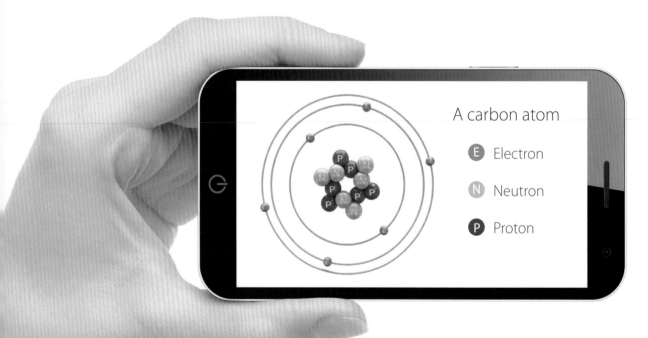

A carbon atom

E Electron

N Neutron

P Proton

Your hand, a smartphone, this book—each one of these things contains carbon atoms.

Charting the Atoms

The periodic table shows all the chemical elements known to exist, and the atoms that make them. Some elements occur naturally. Others are developed in laboratories and are therefore artificial, or human-made. The periodic table lists them in order of increasing atomic number, or the number of protons in the atom's nucleus. Carbon is number 6 in the table.

For example, one of those is carbon, represented on the periodic table as C. Another is oxygen, represented the letter O. When one carbon atom combines with two oxygen atoms, they form a molecule called CO_2. That is carbon dioxide.

In the center of each atom is a **nucleus**, which contains **protons** and **neutrons**. Surrounding the nucleus is a cloud of **electrons**. The number of electrons is the same as the number of protons in an element. Carbon has six protons and six electrons.

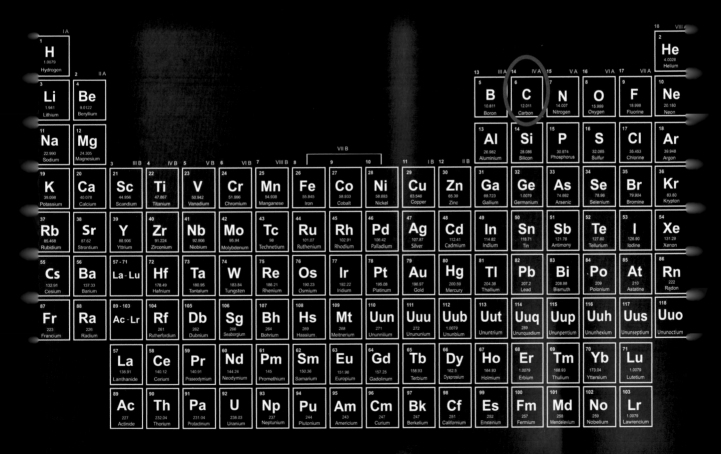

PERIODIC TABLE OF ELEMENTS

Crystal Clear, and Crystal Black

Pure carbon exists on Earth in two forms, and you'd never guess they were different versions of the same thing! One is the hardest natural substance on Earth. The other is one of the softest. One is bright and completely see-through. The other is black and **opaque**, so you can't see through it at all. One is so rare, it is used to make the finest jewelry in the world. The other is so easy to find that it's used to make pencils.

One is called diamond. The other is graphite.

What makes these two forms of carbon so different is the way their individual atoms are arranged. Each form is a **crystal** made up of a repeating pattern of carbon atoms.

The atoms in graphite are joined together in sheets of **hexagons**, or six-sided rings. Each flat sheet, or layer, of hexagons is only loosely bonded to the sheets above and below it. That means it's easy to break those layers apart. This is what makes graphite soft and easy to break. Diamonds, on the other hand, are made of carbon atoms joined in a complicated,

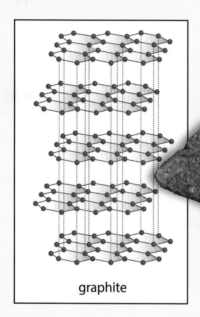

graphite

Loosely bonded carbon atoms (in diagram at left) make natural graphite very soft, just right for leaving marks on paper as the substance we call "pencil lead"!

Carbon Facts and Figures

- The chemical symbol for carbon is C.
- The name "carbon" comes from the Latin word *carbo*, meaning "coal."
- French scientist Antoine Lavoisier named carbon in 1789.
- Carbon is the fourth most common known element in the universe—after hydrogen, helium, and oxygen.
- It is the 15th most common element in Earth's crust.
- It is the second most common element in the human body, after oxygen.
- Humans have known about carbon since ancient times. They first discovered it in charcoal and soot.
- Carbon is created inside stars. It is in the ash left over when stars burn helium.

three dimensional structure. This structure is called a **tetrahedron**. Each carbon atom is joined to four other carbon atoms, and all the tetrahedrons are connected. The bonds between the atoms in these clusters of tetrahedrons are so strong that they are almost impossible to break. That makes diamond the hardest natural substance on the planet.

Carbon is one of about 90 elements, or pure substances, that exist naturally on Earth. But most carbon, including the carbon in your body, is not pure carbon. It is contained in carbon **compounds**. This means that the carbon has bonded, or become joined, with other elements.

Carbon Connections

Carbon may exist in only two *pure* forms, diamond and graphite, but it is an ingredient in about 10 million different carbon compounds. A carbon compound is formed when carbon atoms link with other types of atoms.

One of the most common carbon compound**s** is carbon dioxide, or CO_2. Carbon dioxide is a colorless, odorless gas that is part of the air around us. It is essential to the carbon cycle—and to us! We breathe in oxygen, which reacts with carbon compounds in our bodies, then we breathe out carbon dioxide.

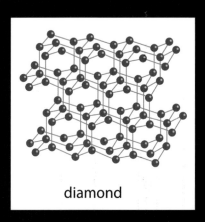

The tight bonds of carbon atoms (left) make diamond the hardest natural substance on Earth—so hard that diamonds are cut along the layers of atoms, not across them.

diamond

Carbon monoxide, or CO, is also a clear, colorless gas. It is also present, in relatively tiny amounts, in our air. Volcanoes produce carbon monoxide when they erupt. It can also be produced by burning wood or substances such as charcoal, gasoline, coal, and other fuels. Unlike carbon dioxide, though, this carbon compound can be deadly when we breathe it in concentrated amounts or in enclosed spaces!

Carbon is found in plants in compounds called carbohydrates. **Carbohydrates** are made of carbon, hydrogen, and oxygen atoms. Another type of carbon compound, called calcium carbonate, is found in some types of rock, such as limestone. It is also the main ingredient in eggshells, seashells, pearls, coral reefs, and chalk.

The gases spewing out of this volcano in Japan include carbon monoxide (CO) and carbon dioxide (CO_2). While both CO and CO_2 can be deadly in above-normal quantities, carbon dioxide normally exists in our atmosphere in amounts that are perfect for the exchange of gases by different life forms.

Carbon is everywhere on Earth, and it's crucial to all known life forms. In fact, there are more things that contain carbon than things that don't, and it's the carbon cycle that makes sure it gets everywhere it's needed!

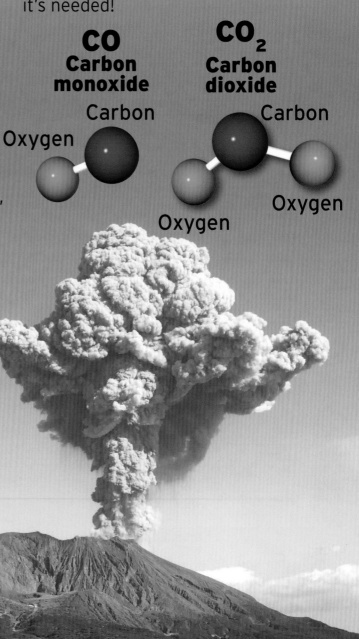

CO
Carbon monoxide
Carbon
Oxygen

CO_2
Carbon dioxide
Carbon
Oxygen
Oxygen

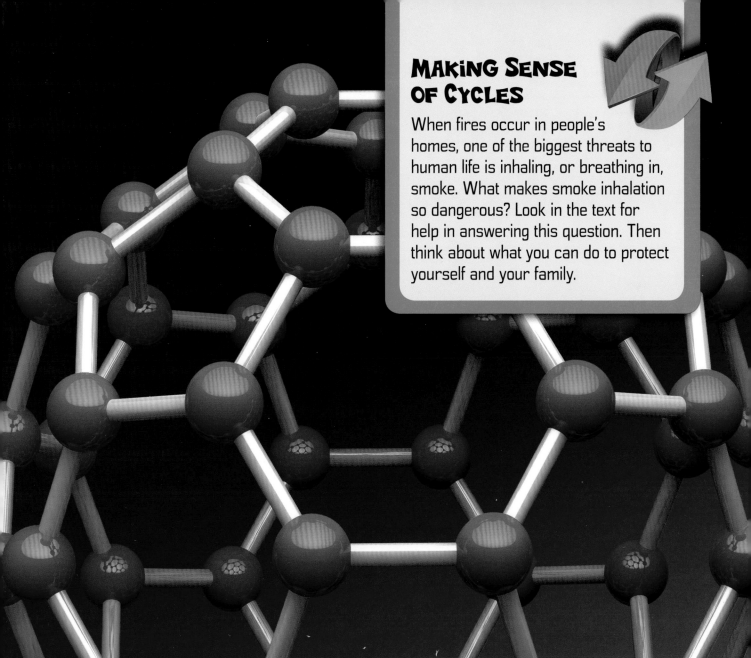

MAKING SENSE OF CYCLES

When fires occur in people's homes, one of the biggest threats to human life is inhaling, or breathing in, smoke. What makes smoke inhalation so dangerous? Look in the text for help in answering this question. Then think about what you can do to protect yourself and your family.

Carbon from Outer Space

For years, scientists had been studying strange carbon molecules that were detected in outer space. In 1985, a trio of British chemists found a way to produce one such molecule in the lab. The new particle was made of 60 carbon atoms, and it looked like a soccer ball!

The scientists called their new discovery Buckminsterfullerene, in honor of U.S. architect and author Buckminster Fuller. The C_{60} molecule looked like the **geodesic domes** that Fuller famously used in his architecture. Several similar molecules (like the model shown here) have now been discovered. All are hollow balls or tubes of carbon atoms. This class of molecules is called Fullerenes.

CHAPTER 2

Cycles Make the World Go 'Round

We've all heard the question: Which came first, the chicken or the egg? A chicken lays an egg. The egg hatches a baby chick. The chick grows up to be a chicken. That chicken lays an egg, which hatches a baby chick, which grows up . . . and so on. The chicken-and-egg question is an example of a cycle, a pattern of related processes or events that happens over and over again. Like a circle, a cycle has no beginning or end. It just keeps going and going and going . . .

Cycles of Life

Every day, our planet performs many cycles. In fact, every day *is* a cycle. As Earth rotates, or spins, the cycle of day and night occurs. During the day, your little place on Earth moves away from the Sun, and day turns to night. During the night, your place on Earth moves back toward the Sun, and night turns to day.

Some of Earth's natural cycles are less easy to notice, and many happen without us even knowing about them. Some occur at such a **microscopic** level that we can't see them. One such cycle is the carbon cycle. We can't see it happening, but we can't live without it.

As Earth rotates on its axis and orbits around the Sun, two familiar cycles occur.

Right: As Earth rotates, the cycle of day and night occurs. During the day, your little place on Earth moves away from the Sun, and day turns to night. During the night, we can watch another part of the cycle—the Moon moving in its path around Earth.

Below: Spring, summer, fall, and winter. The changing of the seasons is a cycle that happens over and over again, year after year.

SPRING
New shoots appear on the tree's branches and develop into leaves.

WINTER
The tree rests in readiness for the cycle to begin again in spring.

A tree goes through a cycle each year with the changing seasons.

SUMMER
Using water, carbon dioxide, and sunlight, the tree's leaves make food for the tree.

FALL
With less sunlight available to make food, the tree's leaves drop to save energy.

The Carbon Cycle

As a natural element that cannot be created or destroyed, all the carbon that exists on the planet is recycled, used over and over again in a variety of forms.

Every known living thing needs some form of carbon to stay alive. Every living thing is also part of the carbon cycle that moves this essential element everywhere it is needed. Carbon travels from the air to plants, to animals, and back to the air. Soil and water also play important roles in the carbon cycle.

For millions of years, the carbon cycle has gone on in perfect balance. In the last 200 years, though, the cycle has started losing its balance. Human activities have been upsetting the cycle's natural

MAKING SENSE OF CYCLES

What cycles do you experience in your daily life? Using examples from this book and your own life, keep a list of cycles that can happen in your body and in the environment around you. How do these cycles affect you? What might happen if the circle were "to break" in any of these cycles?

harmony, and that could lead to all kinds of problems for life on Earth.

Understanding the importance of carbon and a balanced carbon cycle will help us keep us and our planet healthy. Because the carbon cycle is a *cycle*, it doesn't have a beginning or an end point. But we have to start somewhere, so let's start with plants!

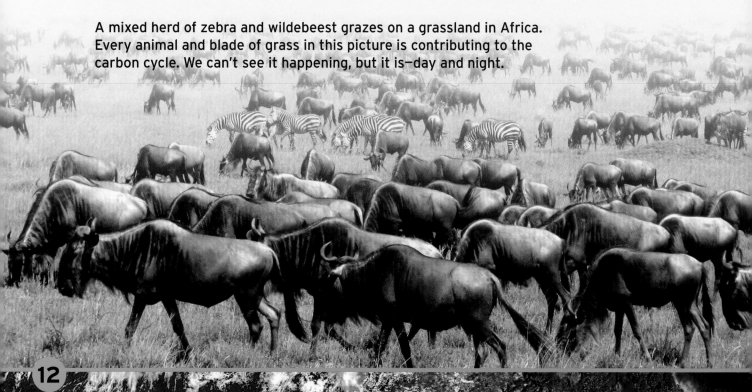

A mixed herd of zebra and wildebeest grazes on a grassland in Africa. Every animal and blade of grass in this picture is contributing to the carbon cycle. We can't see it happening, but it is—day and night.

Carbon Spheres

Carbon exists as carbon dioxide in our **atmosphere**, the layer of air and gases that surrounds Earth. On land, carbon supports life in the **biosphere**, which is made of plant and animal **ecosystems**. It does this by creating energy-giving compounds. In rivers, lakes, and oceans, which make up Earth's **hydrosphere**, the carbon cycle is essential to the survival of marine life. It also helps certain sea creatures build protective shells.

The carbon cycle also reaches into the depths of Earth's **geosphere**. That's the solid part of the planet. It includes rocks, mountains, desert sand, the ocean floor, and everything below Earth's surface. Carbon has been collecting in deep underground pockets for millions of years. Humankind is now harvesting this carbon as a source of energy.

Carbon is critical to the survival of aquatic life throughout Earth's hydrosphere. Shown here are fish and other organisms living in, on, and around a coral reef in the Red Sea near the Middle East.

Carbon helps keep the protective outer shells or exoskeletons of many ocean creatures, such as this stone crab, tough and strong.

CHAPTER 3

The Carbon Cycle in Plants

Plants are amazing things. They pull out of thin air almost everything they need to survive! With just sunshine and carbon dioxide (CO_2), along with some water mixed in, they make their own food. What's even more amazing is that plants then blend all those things together to produce something nearly every member of the animal kingdom needs to survive—oxygen. From the smallest ant to the largest elephant, from lobsters in the sea to birds in the air, from the lowly earthworm to people like you and me—we all need oxygen to breathe.

Sun + Water + CO_2 = Food in Plants

The process that green plants use to convert water, sunlight, and carbon dioxide into food is called **photosynthesis**. The first step for the plant is to collect all the required raw materials.

The plant's roots absorb water from the soil. That water travels up the stem and out to the leaves.

At the same time that the leaves are drawing water from within the plant, they are also collecting carbon dioxide from the air around the plant. Carbon dioxide enters the leaves through tiny holes called **stomata**. Meanwhile, a chemical in the leaves called **chlorophyll** absorbs sunlight. This completes the list of ingredients the plant needs to grow.

Stomata

A greatly enlarged photo, taken by an electron microscope, showing stomata on the leaf of a potato plant.

A Word About Photosynthesis

- The word *photosynthesis* comes from Greek root words meaning light (*photo*) and combining (*synthesis*).
- U.S. scientist Charles Barnes was the first to use the word in 1893.

Sunlight

Oxygen

Carbon dioxide

Water

Sunlight, carbon dioxide, and water: the three main ingredients a green plant needs to produce its own food through photosynthesis. In the process, the plant also releases oxygen into the air.

Now that all three ingredients—water, carbon dioxide, and sunlight—have arrived in the leaves, photosynthesis can start. Here's how it works:

The chlorphyll in the plant's leaves absorbs energy from the Sun.

That energy powers a chemical reaction that breaks up water and carbon dioxide molecules. The reaction also rearranges the molecules to produce a type of sugar called **glucose**. This reaction also produces oxygen. The oxygen, or O_2, is released into the air.

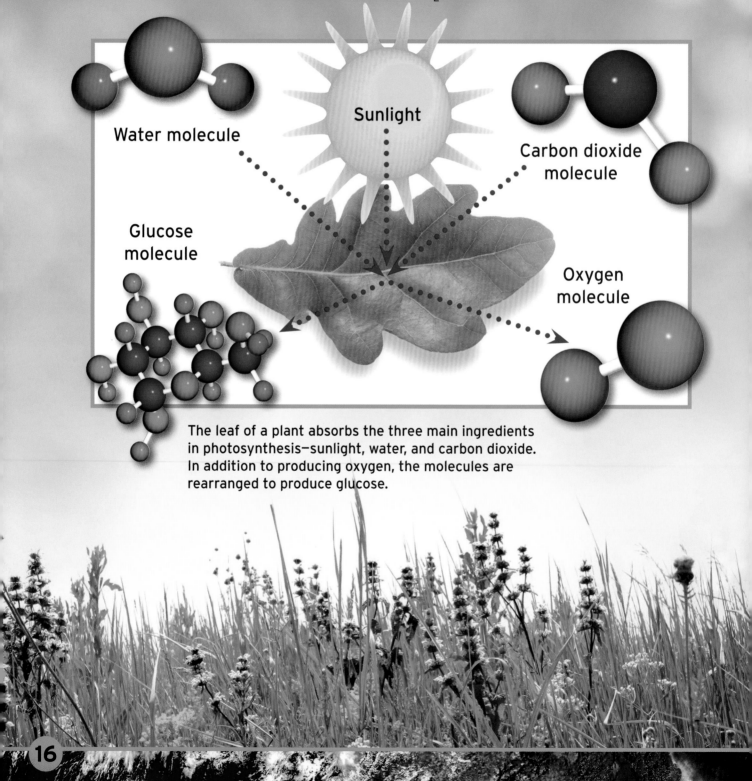

Sunlight

Water molecule

Carbon dioxide molecule

Glucose molecule

Oxygen molecule

The leaf of a plant absorbs the three main ingredients in photosynthesis—sunlight, water, and carbon dioxide. In addition to producing oxygen, the molecules are rearranged to produce glucose.

In the late 1600s, a Belgian doctor conducted experiments to discover where plants got their food. He didn't quite figure it out, but he knew water was key to the process. About 100 years later, a British scientist figured out that plants somehow change the composition of the air around them. Nine years after that, a Dutch doctor discovered that it was only the green parts of plants that could make and absorb the gases that convert and use parts of the air around them. He also discovered that light was the other ingredient necessary for photosynthesis.

Before long, this doctor also suggested that plants release oxygen. It took a Swiss botanist, or plant scientist, to show that the gas plants absorbed from the air was carbon dioxide, or CO_2. Soon afterward, a Swiss chemist put it all together. He showed that plants convert CO_2, plus water, plus light, into oxygen and carbon compounds (sugars). The oxygen is released into the air as a gas. The carbon compounds stay in the plants.

It would take another century—and dozens more researchers—to prove that the oxygen released during photosynthesis actually comes from water, not the CO_2. The oxygen, or O_2, molecules in the CO_2 end up providing nutrition to the plants.

The glucose produced in the leaves feeds the plant. This helps the plant grow, make seeds, and produce fruit and flowers. Usually, a plant produces more glucose than it needs right away. The plant therefore stores the rest for later, in its roots, stems, flowers, seeds, and fruits. The plant dips into this supply of sugar to reproduce and create the next generation of plant life.

Plants also use the stored food when growing conditions are poor. For example, during the winter, the temperatures are lower and days are shorter. During this time of year, trees lose their leaves, and photosynthesis stops. Throughout the rest of the year, however, the trees have stored enough food to survive the winter and to sprout new leaves the following spring.

Planted in the Carbon Cycle

Meanwhile, the oxygen that plants produce during photosynthesis keeps us—and nearly all other animals—alive. We animals in turn convert the oxygen that we inhale into carbon dioxide, which we then exhale. Plants absorb this newly formed carbon dioxide, and the cycle continues.

By clearing carbon dioxide out of our air and replacing it with oxygen, green plants help keep these two gases in perfect balance in our atmosphere. Unfortunately, however, human activity is disturbing this natural balance. As we cut down forests and pave over farmland, we remove air-cleaning trees and plants from Earth. As we burn fuels such as gasoline and coal, carbon dioxide is released into the air, upsetting the natural and ideal balance between carbon dioxide and oxygen in our air.

As Earth's major source of oxygen, plants on land and in water help restore the natural balance. But producing oxygen and clearing the air are not the only ways that plants help us. They are also an important source of food for the animal kingdom, which leads to the next phase of the carbon cycle.

Carbon dioxide

Oxygen

As shown here, plants give off oxygen and animals breathe it in, while animals exhale carbon dioxide and plants absorb it. This exchange of gases is key to the carbon cycle, and to the life forms that depend on it for their survival.

Photosynthesis happens in daylight. But what happens with plants when there's no sunlight to drive this process? What occurs in the absence of sunlight is called **respiration**. Although plants don't breathe, or respire, as we do, they do give off CO_2.

Night and Day

During the day, as part of photosynthesis, plants produce oxygen (O_2) and glucose. Oxygen is released into the atmosphere. Water vapor is also released, during a process called **transpiration**. In the dark, plants rely on stored glucose to provide energy during the night. In that process, called respiration, glucose and oxygen react to produce water vapor and CO_2, which are released into the atmosphere.

As part of the balanced carbon cycle, plants take in far more CO_2 during photosynthesis than they give off during respiration. They also take in a lot less O_2 than they give back. That's a good thing for humans and other animals, because we depend on this balance to provide us with the oxygen we need!

Carbon dioxide   Water vapor   Water vapor   Oxygen

The release of gases from plants during the day and at night. At night, the plant releases carbon dioxide and water vapor into the air in the process called respiration. During the day, it releases oxygen and water vapor in the process known as transpiration.

CHAPTER 4

The Carbon Cycle in Animals

Animals cannot live without plants for two simple reasons.

First of all, green plants produce oxygen, something most organisms need to survive. Whether they do it through lungs, gills, or their skin, nearly all animals take in oxygen, or O_2.

Another element plants supply is carbon, a necessity for all life forms on Earth. Plants deliver carbon in the form of sugars, starches, or proteins. Each of these carbon compounds gives animals, including you, energy for growth, strength, and healthy bodies. Some of the best-known carbon compounds are carbohydrates.

Counting on Carbohydrates

Carbohydrates are molecules made of carbon, oxygen, and hydrogen. Plants produce two types of carbohydrates–simple sugars, and complex carbohydrates.

Glucose, which is produced during photosynthesis, is a simple sugar. In fruit, glucose is converted to a different simple sugar called **fructose**. This is what gives a peach or cherry its sweet taste.

Plants also convert glucose into two different complex carbohydrates. One of these compounds is called **starch**. The other is **cellulose**. Both are made of long chains of glucose molecules fused together.

When plants have more glucose than they need right away, they save it as starch. Starch is stored in roots, seeds, berries, and other plant parts. A potato, for example, is simply a stash of starch the plant is saving for later. When the plant needs energy, it converts the starch back to glucose. Other common sources of starch are corn, wheat, and rice.

The other complex carbohydrate, cellulose, is made of sheets of glucose chains layered on top of each other. Powerful bonds hold the sheets together, making cellulose a strong, stiff building material for plants. They use cellulose to keep their shape, and to keep from falling over. Stems, trunks, and **cell** walls are made of cellulose. Cotton is almost pure cellulose. Wood is about 50 percent cellulose.

Cotton

The tasty baked potato we eat is the plant's enlarged stem, called a tuber.

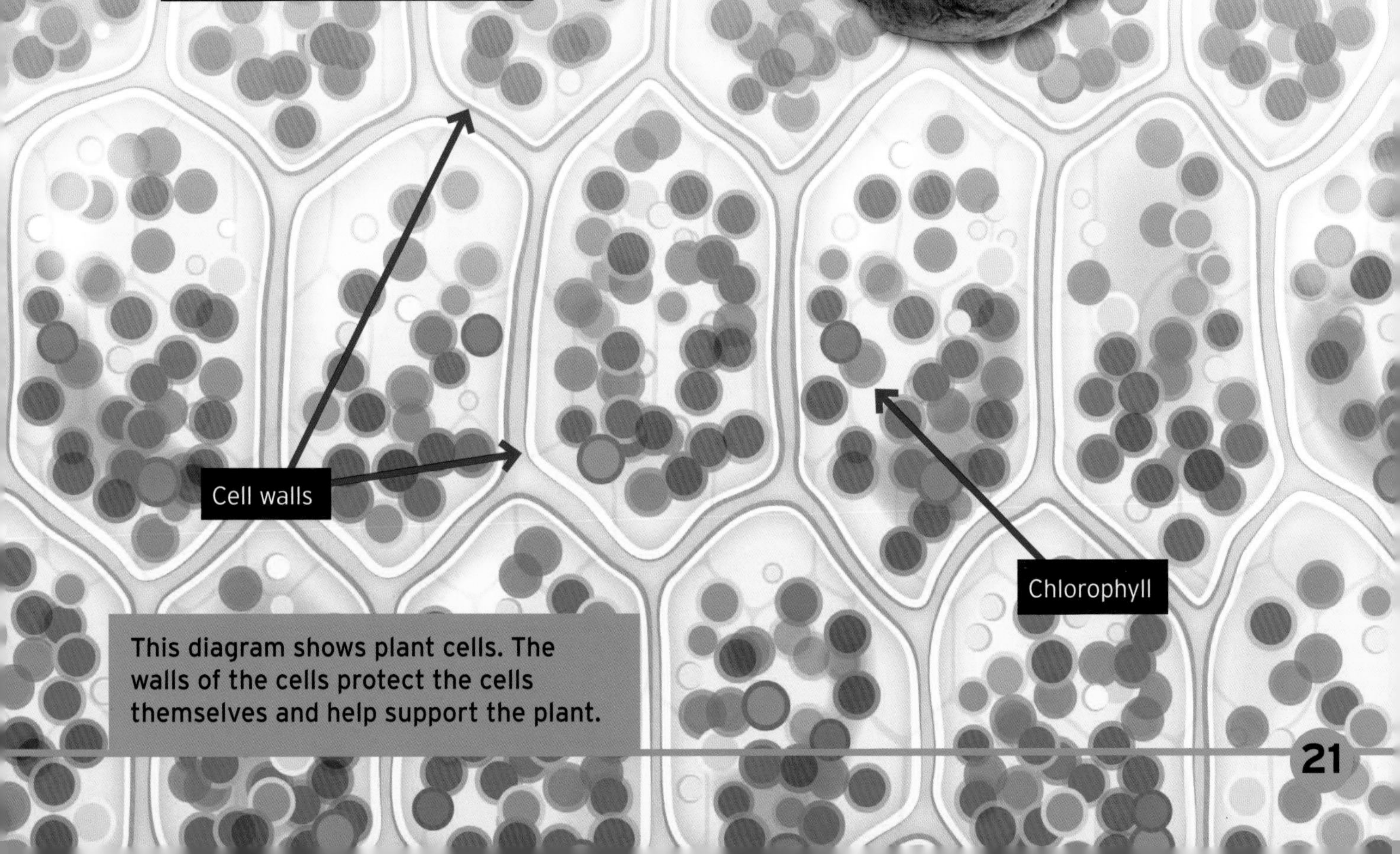

Cell walls

Chlorophyll

This diagram shows plant cells. The walls of the cells protect the cells themselves and help support the plant.

Plants on the Menu

When any animal, whether it's a flamingo, a horse, or even a cricket, eats a plant, it consumes the carbon contained in the sugars, starch, and cellulose of that plant.

Most animals cannot digest cellulose. There are a few, such as termites, cows, and koalas, that have chemicals in their stomachs to break down the cellulose. These chemicals convert cellulose to energy for the animal. In most other organisms, the cellulose passes right through the body and is eliminated as waste. In human food, cellulose is called fiber, and it's an important part of our diet. It keeps our digestive systems working well.

Starch, on the other hand, is a vital source of energy for all organisms. When an animal ingests, or takes in, plant starch as food, chemical reactions start to dissolve the starch into individual glucose molecules.

Certain animals, such as koalas (top), are able to digest cellulose and convert it to energy. Other animals, such as humans, use cellulose as a source of dietary fiber, which helps food pass through our digestive systems.

Carbon Compounded

Pure carbon does not exist in the bodies of humans and other animals. Instead, it forms carbon compounds. These carbon compounds keep these animals alive and thriving.

For example, carbon bonds with calcium and oxygen to form calcium carbonate—the main ingredient in bones and teeth. It is also the main component in the shells of snails, oysters, and other sea-creatures. Turtle shells, on the other hand, are made of a combination of carbon, oxygen, and another element called phosphorus (P).

When carbon blends with atoms of nitrogen (N) and other elements, it forms proteins, which are the building blocks of animal life. Almost every body part of every animal contains some kind of protein. For example, blood, skin, birds' beaks, and deer antlers all contain protein. Some proteins help keep us from getting sick.

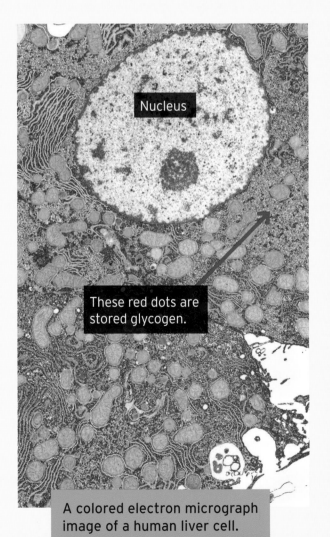

Nucleus

These red dots are stored glycogen.

A colored electron micrograph image of a human liver cell.

This occurs as food is digested in the animal's intestines. From the intestines, glucose molecules are absorbed into the bloodstream. The blood then carries glucose to cells in every part of the body.

Glucose is the fuel that powers life. It helps muscles work, feeds the brain, and drives all bodily functions. Like a plant, if an organism has more glucose than it needs, it stores it for later. Humans store extra glucose in cells of their livers and muscles in chains of glucose molecules. These molecules make up a substance called **glycogen**. The body's cells can only hold so much glycogen, however. Once there is no more room for it to be stored, the glucose is converted into fat.

Ladybugs feed on aphids.

Aphids feed on plants.

Animals get sugars and starches from plants and from animals that eat plants.

MAKING SENSE OF CYCLES

Carbon is crucial to all known life forms on Earth. When the carbon cycle is in balance, it ensures that the right amount of carbon is available for living organisms when they need it. What might cause the carbon cycle to become unbalanced? Then what might happen if its balance is shifted or broken? Support your answer using evidence from what you have read in this book about the carbon cycle in plants and animals.

Some creatures, such as ladybugs, owls, and lions, don't eat plants, but they have adapted to use the food they do eat to get carbohydrates. For example, they eat animals that eat plants, and those plant-eating animals contain the sugars and starches the meat-eaters need.

Take a Deep Breath

As humans and other animals convert glucose into energy, we are an important part of the carbon cycle. When we breathe in oxygen, it circulates through our blood. In our bloodstream, the oxygen mixes with glucose. This helps create the chemical reaction that releases the energy to move, grow, and keep our hearts beating, along with many other functions. The reaction also produces carbon dioxide. Carbon dioxide circulates through our bodies in our bloodstream. It leaves when we exhale, or breathe it out through our lungs.

This process is called respiration. It is the opposite of photosynthesis, in which plants release oxygen into the atmosphere. When we breathe carbon dioxide back into the air, it is available to plants, and the cycle starts all over again!

Carbon may be common, but oxygen is even more abundant in the world. Every known life form on Earth needs carbon to stay alive. Similarly, hardly any living thing, plant or animal, can live without oxygen. It is a component of water and the air we breathe. Here are some other interesting bits of oxygen information:

We Need O₂ Too

- Oxygen is the most common element in the human body. We are 65 percent oxygen. A 100-pound (45-kg) kid contains 65 pounds (29.5 kg) of oxygen. That's about the weight of an average standard poodle!
- Oxygen is the third most abundant element in the universe, after hydrogen and helium.
- In its natural state, oxygen is a colorless, odorless gas.
- Two different scientists discovered oxygen. The first, a Swedish scientist, discovered it in 1772, but he didn't publish his findings. A British scientist discovered it, independently, two years later.

As animals eat and breathe, they contribute to the carbon cycle. One major carbon compound given off by animals, particularly cattle, is methane, which is released whenever they pass gas!

Glucose and oxygen give animals energy and create carbon dioxide, CO_2, inside their bodies.

Animals breathe in oxygen made by plants.

Animals breathe out carbon dioxide.

Animals eat plants and obtain glucose.

Plants absorb carbon dioxide and use it for photosynthesis.

CHAPTER 5

Carbon Cycles in Water

Carbon and the carbon cycle don't only exist on land. They also play crucial roles in the marine world. Some of the steps in the carbon cycle are exactly the same in both places. For example, marine plants such as **phytoplankton** absorb carbon dioxide (CO_2), from the water and release oxygen (O_2). That's photosynthesis, and it's the same process land-based plants use. It just happens to occur in the water. At the same time, fish and other aquatic animals take in oxygen and release carbon dioxide. That's respiration, the same thing land animals do.

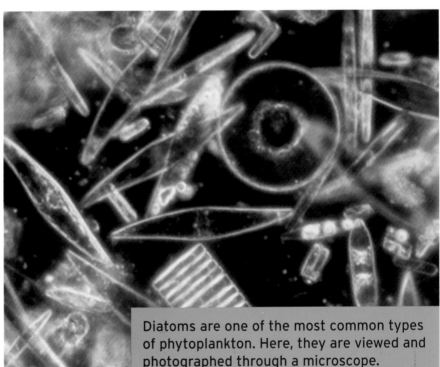

Diatoms are one of the most common types of phytoplankton. Here, they are viewed and photographed through a microscope.

A World of Difference

Some of the steps in the carbon cycle are the same in water as they are on land. There are also, however, some different processes going on only in the oceans. First of all, the carbon dioxide that's floating around in the air has to get into the sea so marine life can use it.

It gets there by dissolving into the upper layer of the water from the air. Once carbon dioxide is dissolved, it may stay as a carbon compound to be used by marine plants in photosynthesis. Or it may combine with other substances and convert to carbon compounds called carbonates and bicarbonates.

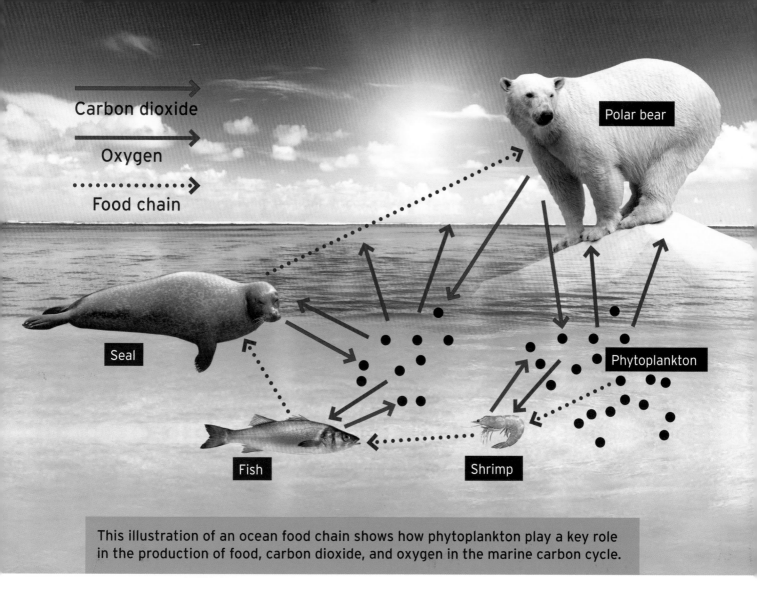

Carbon dioxide

Oxygen

Food chain

Polar bear

Seal

Phytoplankton

Fish

Shrimp

This illustration of an ocean food chain shows how phytoplankton play a key role in the production of food, carbon dioxide, and oxygen in the marine carbon cycle.

Some marine animals, such as oysters, snails, and scallops, use carbonates to build hard, protective shells. First, they absorb carbonates and calcium from the water. Then, through chemical reactions in their bodies, they convert these two elements to calcium carbonate—the main ingredient in seashells.

The most important and the smallest plants in the aquatic carbon cycle are called phytoplankton. Through photosynthesis, these microscopic plants produce *half* the world's oxygen. They are key to keeping carbon dioxide and oxygen levels in balance in our atmosphere.

Phytoplankton are also at the very bottom of the ocean food chain. This means that a lot of animals rely on them for nourishment. Shrimp, for example, eat phytoplankton, then fish eat the shrimp, seals eat the fish, and whales and polar bears eat the seals. That means these microscopic phytoplankton provide oxygen and food for a huge amount of life on Earth—in the water and on land!

Seaside Carbon Facts

- Carbon also enters oceans by traveling down rivers that empty into them. As rivers flow toward the sea, they pick up plant and animal matter along the way. All this carbon-rich material eventually washes into the ocean. There, it becomes part of the marine carbon cycle.
- Waves create more surface area on the water, so rough water takes in more carbon dioxide from the atmosphere than perfectly calm water.
- Cold seawater holds more carbon dioxide than warm water, so water near the North Pole and South Pole absorb carbon dioxide, while water closer to the equator releases carbon dioxide.
- The carbon cycle that happens in oceans also happens in bodies of freshwater such as lakes and rivers. Because only 2.5 percent of Earth's water is freshwater, the high seas play a far greater role in the planet's carbon cycle.

Phytoplankton + Seashells / Sand = Shale rock

Over vast periods of time, dead phytoplankton compress with materials such as seashells and sand at the bottom of the sea. These materials produce carbon-rich deposits of shale and other sedimentary rock.

On top of that, when phytoplankton die, the carbon-rich bodies that don't get eaten fall to the bottom of the sea. There, they are soon covered with other materials that sink to the ocean floor, such as seashells and sand. This eventually builds a layer of **sediment** called a "**carbon sink.**" It's like a garbage dump for carbon.

Over time, some of the carbon compounds at the bottom of the ocean cement with other minerals to form **limestone** and **shale**, two types of sedimentary rock. Some of the carbon, over thousands of years, recycles back to the surface of the water. There, it rejoins the carbon cycle. And some of the carbon-rich material decays as it sits in the sink at the bottom of the sea. This material gets **compressed**, or squeezed, so hard that it eventually becomes **fossil fuel**–coal, oil, or natural gas. This process takes millions of years.

This carbon-to-fuel transformation happens deep within Earth's crust.

Acid Ocean

When carbon dioxide dissolves in the ocean, it reacts with the water to release carbonates and electrically charged hydrogen atoms. These charged atoms are called **ions**. While the carbonates help sea creatures make hard shells, the hydrogen ions make the water more acidic. For thousands of years, nature has made sure that the amount of carbon dioxide (CO_2) and the acidity in the water is just right.

Over the last two centuries, though, humans have added more and more carbon dioxide to the environment, upsetting the balance. Burning fossil fuels to drive cars or to heat homes releases CO_2 into the atmosphere. As the carbon dioxide in the air increases, so does the amount that dissolves into the water. More CO_2 in the water leads to more hydrogen ions in the water. That makes oceans more acidic, and that threatens marine life.

Rising sea temperatures, increasing amounts of CO_2, and other kinds of pollution threaten life in the planet's oceans and seas. This dead coral reef stands in stark contrast to the colorful, vital reef shown on page 13.

CHAPTER 6

The Carbon Cycle Inside Earth

On Earth's surface, plants and animals use photosynthesis and respiration to keep the carbon cycle going and in balance. These processes happen in oceans and lakes, too. There are also parts of the carbon cycle that only happen in water. Underground, and deep below the ocean floor, the carbon cycle continues in still more ways.

Carbon in the Crust

When a plant dies, its greenery decays, or rots. Eventually, it dissolves into the ground. For example, when a green leaf on a maple tree dies in autumn, it turns brown. Then it falls from the tree and settles onto the forest floor. Eventually, it breaks down and becomes part of the soil. This process is called decomposition.

When an animal dies, another animal might eat parts of it. Some bits, such as bones, are left to decompose, or rot. Animals also produce waste, which they leave behind on the land. In lakes and oceans, decaying plant and animal matter, along with waste material, fall to the bottom.

Over time, on land and under water, all this decaying plant

and animal material gets buried deep underground. There, it breaks down into its basic components. Because plant and animal bodies are so rich with carbon compounds, these areas deep within Earth become carbon sinks.

Over hundreds of millions of years, the heat and pressure of Earth's crust converts this buried carbon into fossil fuels—coal, oil, and natural gas. These fossil fuels are excellent sources of energy, so humans dig and drill deep into Earth and the ocean floor to harvest them.

HOW OIL AND GAS FORMED

1. Sea plants and animals die and decay on the seabed.

2. Over time, the remains are buried by layers of sand and other soils. Heat and pressure turn them into oil and gas.

3. Today, we extract oil and gas from under the ground.

HOW COAL FORMED

1. Plants die and settle on the bottoms of swamps, where they decay.

2. Over millions of years, the plant remains are covered by layers of soil and water.

3. Heat and pressure turn the plant remains into coal. Today, we mine the coal from underground.

Driving Force

Just as certain carbon compounds, such as glucose, give energy to plants and animals, other types of carbon compounds provide fuel for other processes. That's why oil, natural gas, and coal-mining companies work hard to **extract**, or remove, fossil fuels from under the surface of the planet.

Oil in its natural state, called crude oil, is a smelly yellow, brown, or black liquid that collects in underground pockets, or reservoirs. It can be refined into gasoline for cars, jet fuel for planes, or propane to fire up the grill. It is also used to make such products as ink, crayons, deodorant, and tires.

MAKING SENSE OF CYCLES

The carbon cycle plays a key role in maintaining balance in the natural world between oxygen and carbon dioxide, as well as among other substances. Based on what you have read about the carbon cycle in water and on Earth, list at least five reasons why balance is so important on our planet. Support your ideas in the list with examples from the book.

Below: From crayons to fuel and the flame on a stove, it's easy to take for granted the many uses of oil-based products in our daily lives.

Some of Earth's coal is close enough to the surface that miners can reach it by digging enormous pits like the one shown here. Supplies like this may be huge and relatively easy to mine, but they do not exist in endless quantities.

Natural gas is used to heat homes, and to power gas fireplaces, water heaters, and stoves. It is a main energy source for power plants that produce electricity. This colorless, odorless gas is also an ingredient in such things as fertilizer, plastics, medicines, and explosives.

Coal is another major source of energy used to make electricity. Like natural gas, coal is burned to heat water in a boiler. When the water gets hot enough, it becomes steam, which powers generators that make electricity. In its natural state, coal is a black rock. It is found in seams, or mines, that are sometimes so close to Earth's surface that miners can get at the coal by digging a big pit. To reach deeper coal beds, miners dig tunnels underground.

It may appear that our Earth holds endless supplies of oil, natural gas, and coal. This is not true.

When a volcano erupts, it blasts gases, ash, and lava, or hot melted rock, into the air. One of the gases that shoots out the top of one of these exploding mountains is carbon dioxide (CO_2). Other than animal respiration, volcanoes are the main natural source of carbon dioxide on Earth. A single volcano may spew masses of carbon dioxide into the air, but it's not enough to upset the natural balance of gases in the atmosphere. Human activities release *100 times* more carbon dioxide every year than all the world's volcanoes put together.

In fact, these supplies are called **non-renewable resources** because, once we've used up the existing supplies, that's the end of them. It takes millions of years for Earth's natural cycles to produce fossil fuels. They cannot be replaced anytime soon.

The reason we rely so heavily on fossil fuels today is that they are relatively cheap to produce. The downside of using these fuels, though, is that burning them releases carbon dioxide into the atmosphere. The more fossil fuels we burn, the more carbon dioxide enters the air. This throws off the natural balance of carbon dioxide and oxygen, which in turn could threaten all living things on the planet.

A coal-fired electrical power plant in Utah.

Carbon travels from the atmosphere to plants and animals, then back into the atmosphere. Soil, water, and actions going on beneath Earth's surface play an important role in the movement of carbon. Human activities also contribute to this process, which is known as the carbon cycle.

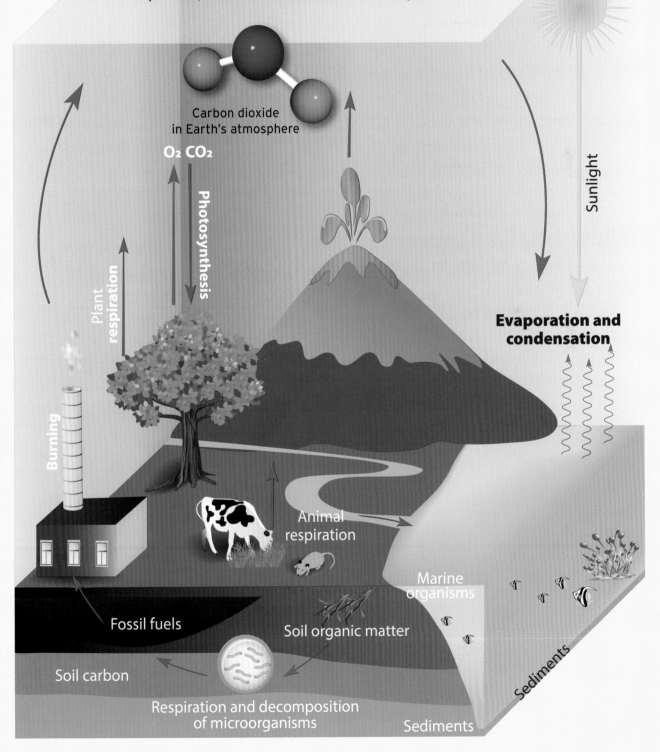

Carbon dioxide in Earth's atmosphere

O_2 CO_2

Photosynthesis

Plant respiration

Burning

Sunlight

Evaporation and condensation

Animal respiration

Fossil fuels

Soil organic matter

Marine organisms

Soil carbon

Respiration and decomposition of microorganisms

Sediments

Sediments

CHAPTER 7

Messing with the C-Cycle

For millions of years, the carbon cycle has kept itself in perfect balance. As carbon moves through the cycle, it creates compounds that give life and energy to plants and animals. It reacts with other elements to create just the right mix of oxygen and carbon dioxide (CO_2) in the atmosphere. It also converts plant and animal waste materials into usable compounds. In the last 200 years or so, though, human activities have begun to disturb this perfectly balanced cycle.

Upsetting the Balance

In today's world, humankind depends on fossil fuels to operate machinery, to heat factories and homes, and to power many types of transportation. When they burn, these fuels release carbon dioxide into our air.

The more cars we drive, electricity we produce, and gadgets we make in factories, the more fossil fuels are burned and the more carbon dioxide goes into our atmosphere. In the last 50 years, the rate of carbon dioxide released into our air has skyrocketed.

Next to using fossil fuels to generate electricity, automotive exhaust is the second-largest source of excess carbon dioxide in Earth's atmosphere.

Clearing forests for their land and lumber has affected the balance between oxygen and carbon dioxide in places like these rain forests in Thailand (above) and Borneo (left).

At the same time, we have been cutting down forests and clearing farmland to create more space for homes, cities, and roads. This leaves the planet with fewer green plants to clean excess carbon dioxide out of the air and release life-giving oxygen in its place.

In short, human activities are throwing the carbon cycle dangerously out of balance.

Earth's atmosphere has always contained gases, including carbon dioxide, that keep the planet warm and able to support life. When the proportions, or balance, of those gases change, though, all life forms are at risk.

When the concentration of carbon dioxide increases, Earth's atmosphere starts to act like a greenhouse. Just like a garden greenhouse, the atmosphere traps more and more of the Sun's heat. Also like a greenhouse, the temperature inside our atmosphere becomes warmer than it would naturally be. This is called **climate change**.

Warmer temperatures mean glaciers and polar ice caps melt. If the ice caps melt, the oceans will rise. This puts coastal towns and sea-level ecosystems at risk of flooding. Warmer waters threaten cool-water-loving phytoplankton, which supply half the world's oxygen.

Higher temperatures may also lead to droughts, or dry spells. This means that crops can't grow properly, and food could become scarce. To survive the changing climate, plants and animals around the world have already begun to adapt or move to new habitats.

Rising global temperatures also lead to unusual weather patterns and natural disasters. They may not appear to be related to global warming, but they are. Hurricanes, wildfires, heat waves, and severe lightning storms are all related to climate change. Other potential long-term impacts include seasons changing at different times of year than usual, animals becoming extinct, and a decreasing supply of fresh water.

Right: These images, based on satellite views of Earth from space, show the reduced extent of Arctic sea ice between summer 1984 (left) and summer 2012 (right).

A fire-fighting helicopter over a forest fire in Northern California, August 2014. A lack of rainfall and high temperatures have created dangerous conditions in California for several years.

Rebalancing the Cycle

For years, scientists and engineers have been working to find ways to reduce humans' use of fossil fuels, and therefore reduce the CO_2 in our air. The goal is to halt, or at least slow down, climate change.

Some researchers are developing electric cars, airplanes that run on solar power, and trains that are pulled along their tracks by magnetic forces rather than being driven by diesel fuel. Others are looking into new, and renewable, sources of fuel. Green algae, for example, could be an excellent, easy-to-grow **biofuel**, or fuel from living sources. Wind power and the rise and fall of tides are also being studied as potential energy sources.

Some engineers are finding new ways to build homes and factories that use less energy. Certain manufacturers are developing products made from recycled or plant-based materials, rather than using materials made from petroleum-based resources.

MAKING SENSE OF CYCLES

The amount of CO_2 in the air has increased by **36** percent in the last 250 years because of burning fossil fuels. It took the first 200 years for half of that extra CO_2 to enter our atmosphere—and only the last 50 years for the rest of it to get there! What do those numbers tell us about the rate at which we are using fossil fuels and adding CO_2 to Earth's atmosphere? Find other information in this book about CO_2 in the atmosphere to help support your thinking.

A worker in France tends to ponds being used to grow algae. Like plants, algae use photosynthesis to produce their own food and contribute to the exchange of oxygen and carbon dioxide in the atmosphere. They can grow in just about any kind of water, even sewage, and are an excellent source of biofuel.

If these actions are not enough to stop climate change, climate engineers may have to step in. Climate engineering, also called **geoengineering**, refers to activities designed to artificially change Earth's climate. That could include such things as sending mirrors into space to bounce some of the Sun's rays away from Earth. It could also include adding light-reflecting particles to the air to redirect sunlight, or fertilizing oceans to increase the amount of CO_2 phytoplankton can absorb.

Geoengineers are also looking into ways to remove CO_2 from the atmosphere and store it underground. All these geoengineering activities may have unwanted consequences and they are very expensive. So far, none have been tested.

Hopefully, we won't have to start messing with the Sun's rays and ocean water to stop climate change. The best thing we can do right now is reduce, reuse, and recycle to cut our use of fossil fuels. That is the first step to helping the carbon cycle get back in balance and keep the planet healthy.

This art shows an array of giant mirrors launched into orbit above Earth. (Note the Moon at left.) The purpose of the mirrors would be to reflect sunlight away from Earth and reduce global warming. Such a project would come at a high cost and with uncertain results. It would probably be considered only if other efforts to restore balance to the carbon cycle failed.

Your **carbon footprint** is the amount of carbon dioxide you create during your day-to-day activities. The smaller your carbon footprint, the better it will be for the planet!

For example, if you leave all the lights on in your home when you go out, your carbon footprint will be greater than if you turn all the lights off. While electricity doesn't release carbon dioxide, the fossil fuels needed to create electricity do. Power plants that create electricity are the biggest producers of carbon dioxide on Earth! Using less electricity will instantly reduce your carbon footprint.

Heating a home, driving a car that runs on gasoline, and using products that are shipped from far away are other activities that increase your carbon footprint. Here are some ideas to help you help the planet by reducing your carbon footprint:

- Decide what you'd like to eat before you open the refrigerator, so the fridge door doesn't stand open and waste electricity.
- Help adults plan their errands, so they travel the shortest distance possible in the car.
- Choose locally made products and locally produced food. This will reduce the distance these items have to travel in carbon dioxide-producing trucks, ships, or airplanes.
- Plant a garden. Plants help clean carbon dioxide out of the air. Also, if you grow food, it doesn't need to be shipped anywhere. (Plus, homegrown fruits and vegetables usually taste better than the store-bought kind!)
- Turn off the TV when you're finished watching it. Unplug the iPod or phone charger when the device is charged.
- Check your sinks for dripping faucets. Wasting water also wastes the energy needed to pump and purify it. Dripping hot water also wastes the energy needed to heat the water.
- Steer clear of drive-throughs. Sitting in the car with the engine running pumps carbon dioxide into the air. Instead, park the car and go inside to place your order.
- Avoid bottled water. The companies that bottle it use energy and produce carbon dioxide, and so do the factories that make the bottles. On top of that, bottled water has to be shipped to the store where you buy it. This produces even more CO_2.
- Shop at thrift stores so you can reuse clothing (and get great deals!). New clothes are made in factories and use processes that produce carbon dioxide.

Back to the Soil

All living things contain carbon, even after they die. Their remains break down, or decompose, releasing the carbon. Much of the work of decomposition is carried out by bacteria and fungi living in the soil. Some of the released carbon goes into the atmosphere. Some stays in the soil in the humus, or organic material. You can't see it, but it's there! Carbon may stay in the soil for millions of years. Natural gas and oil began millions of years ago as decaying carbon-rich plants and animals.

So is it possible to observe the effects of living organisms breaking down carbon-rich plant material in soil?

In this activity, you will observe and compare decomposition of plant material and nonliving objects in the soil.

You Will Need

- Dishpan or large bucket
- Enough soil to fill the dishpan or bucket (if possible, use soil from a garden, yard, or vacant lot rather than packaged potting soil)
- Mesh bag such as one that fresh produce (oranges, onions, potatoes) is sold in
- Spray bottle with water
- Several different plant materials, such as a dead leaf or a fresh leaf, a flower, a fresh piece of soft vegetable or fruit (tomato, apple, grape, berry, green pepper), an orange section, or a piece of orange peel
- Several nonliving objects, such as a penny, a small plastic object, and a pebble
- 6 paper plates (enough to use one every few days for about two weeks)
- Rubber band
- Ruler
- Scissors
- 6 toothpicks (enough to use one every few days for about two weeks)
- Newspapers (optional)
- Notebook or pad of paper and pen or pencil

Instructions

1 Work outdoors if possible. If not, cover your work area with newspaper.

2 Fill dishpan or bucket with soil at least 4-6 inches (10-15 cm) deep.

3 Spray the soil so that it is moist but not soggy, and mix it up.

4 Cut the piece of mesh roughly 6 x 6 inches (15 cm) square and spread it out on the plate.

5 Put both plant and nonliving materials in the center of the mesh.

6 Gather together the corners and edges of the mesh to form a bag around the materials. Use a rubber band to keep the opening of the bag closed tightly.

7 Bury the bag so that the materials are completely under the soil, but leave the neck of the bag poking out of the surface.

8 Spray the soil every day as needed to keep it moist.

9 After three days, dig up the bag and carefully empty the contents onto a paper plate. Use a toothpick to spread out the contents. Separate the materials so that signs of breaking down among the individual items are easier to spot.

10 Examine the materials for evidence of decomposition among the various items. Look to see whether certain items tend to decompose faster than others, or whether certain parts of an item tend to decompose more slowly. Take notes, recording what you observe.

11 Put everything back into the bag, close it with the rubber band, and bury it again.

12 Repeat every three days for about two weeks. Be sure to record your observations in your notebook.

The Challenge

After two weeks, present your investigation to others, explaining what you did and what you have discovered. Think about and discuss:

- What changes you have observed and why they happened.
- How these changes are related to the carbon in the materials you buried.
- What has happened to the carbon that was in the living plants.
- How decomposition of living things is part of the larger carbon cycle.

atoms The basic unit of a chemical element. Atoms make up all living and nonliving things

biosphere All the regions of the land, water, and air occupied by living organisms on Earth

biofuel A renewable fuel made from plant or animal sources, such as corn or animal waste

carbohydrates Molecules made of carbon, oxygen, and hydrogen that provide energy for all living things

carbon footprint The way of measuring how much carbon dioxide (CO_2) a person, building, or business is responsible for releasing into the atmosphere through such daily activities as driving a car or using electricity

carbon sink A place in nature where excess carbon is stored; often the carbon comes from waste plant and animal matter

cells Basic, microscopic parts of an organism, consisting of a membrane, or skin, enclosing a nucleus and material known as cytoplasm

cellulose Molecules made from long chains of glucose molecules that provide structure to plants

chlorophyll A green chemical in plant leaves that is responsible for absorbing light to provide energy from the Sun for the process of photosynthesis

compound Atoms and molecules that bond together to form a new substance

climate change A process in which the environment becomes warmer, colder, drier, or wetter than normal. This can occur naturally or can be caused by human activity.

condensation The process of converting, or changing, a substance from a gaseous state to a liquid state. For example, when water vapor condenses, it becomes liquid water.

crystal A solid structure in which the atoms are joined in a three-dimensional, repeating pattern

electron A tiny, negatively charged particle of energy in an atom

ecosystem A community of organisms and the environment that they share and in which they interact

element A pure chemical substance. Each element contains only one type of atom

evaporation The process of converting, or changing, a liquid substance to a gaseous state. For example, when water evaporates, it becomes water vapor.

extract To remove, often with effort

fossil fuel A fuel source that began as organisms or plant material buried deep beneath Earth's surface and underwent decomposition and other natural processes, usually over periods of millions of years, and were eventually converted to oil, coal, or natural gas

fructose The simple sugar in fruit

geodesic dome A three-dimensional ball made of interlocking, flat, multi-sided shapes

geoengineering The use of scientific methods and techniques to alter the environment on a large scale in an effort to reduce the effects of greenhouse gases and climate change

geosphere The solid parts of Earth, including rocks and mountains above ground and Earth's crust and core below ground

glucose A simple sugar that provides energy for all living things

glycogen Molecules made from long chains of glucose molecules stored in animals' bodies

hydrosphere All the water on Earth's surface, such as lakes, rivers, and seas; sometimes includes water above Earth's surface in the form of clouds

ion A positively or negatively charged atom or molecule

limestone A type of rock composed mainly of calcium carbonate

microscopic So small as to be visible only with a microscope

molecule A particle formed when two or more atoms bond together

neutron A neutral particle found in the nucleus of an atom

non-renewable resource A resource whose supply doesn't refresh quickly enough to be used again

nucleus The dense center of an atom; contains protons and neutrons

opaque Not able to be seen through; not transparent

periodic table A table that shows all known chemical elements in order of atomic number, or the number of protons in the atom's nucleus

photosynthesis A process by which plants convert carbon dioxide, water, and sunlight into oxygen and sugars

phytoplankton Tiny marine plants that produce half the world's oxygen

proton A positively charged particle in the nucleus of an atom

respiration The process by which organisms convert oxygen and sugars into carbon dioxide and water. This process is the reverse of what happens in photosynthesis, in which plants convert carbon dioxide, water, and sunlight into oxygen and sugars

sediment Loose materials, including plant and animal residue and pieces of rock and sand, that settle to the bottom of a liquid and layer on top of each other

shale Layered rock formed, over long periods of time, from sediments at the bottom of oceans and other bodies of water. Black shale contains much organic, carbon-rich material

starch Molecules made from long chains of glucose molecules, they provide energy to plants and animals

stomata (singular: *stoma*) Tiny holes, or pores, on a leaf that allow the leaf to absorb gases such as carbon dioxide from the air around it and give off gases such as water vapor and oxygen

tetrahedron A three-dimensional shape that looks like a pyramid

transpiration Giving off water vapor through stomata in the leaves of a plant

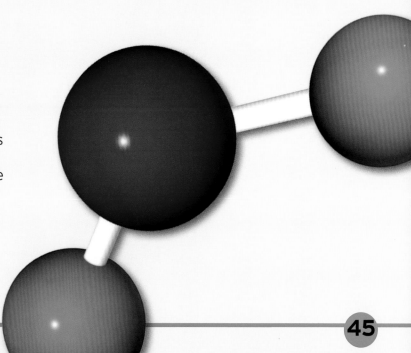

BOOKS

Silverstein, Alvin, and Virginia B. Silverstein, and Laura Silverstein Nunn. *Photosynthesis*. (Science Concepts) Twenty-First Century Books, 2008.

Slade, Suzanne. *The Carbon Cycle*. (Cycles in Nature) PowerKids Press, 2007.

Sparrow, Giles. *Carbon*. (The Elements) Cavendish Square, 1999.

WEBSITES

climatekids.nasa.gov/menu/carbons-travels/
Carbon's Travels is an excellent online resource with games, puzzles, photos, and interactive graphics related to the carbon cycle. The main website, called *Climate Kids: NASA's Eyes on the Earth*, features superb sections on other climate-related topics, such as energy, technology, ocean, and air.

www.epa.gov/climatechange/kids/basics/today/carbon-dioxide.html
All About Carbon Dioxide features a great video explaining the carbon cycle. Click on the Greenhouse Effect link to find another excellent video. Another page on this website gives lots of ideas about how you can reduce your carbon footprint: www.epa.gov/climatechange/kids/solutions/actions/index.html

cO3.apogee.net/contentplayer/?coursetype=kids&utilityid=entergyela&id=16174
This is a weird website address, but it's a good website! This links directly to a page about the carbon cycle. Under the *Energy & Environment* heading in the menu, you'll also find links titled "Greenhouse Gases," "What's up with Carbon?" and "Driving CO_2 Production." Under the *Let's Explore Energy* heading, you'll find more information about two fossil fuels–coal and natural gas.

www.eia.gov/KIDS/energy.cfm?page=2
Energy Kids is a site with lots of information about different energy sources. Learn about the non-renewable, carbon-based fossil fuels, along with some good news about new, more environmentally friendly energy sources. Check out the *Games and Activities* section to find energy-related jokes, or to take a virtual field trip to an oil refinery or wind turbine.

ABOUT THE AUTHOR

Diane Dakers was born and raised in Toronto and now makes her home
in Victoria, British Columbia, Canada. She has been a newspaper, television,
and radio journalist since 1991. She participates in the carbon cycle by breathing
air, planting a garden, eating lots of fruits and vegetables, and working
hard to reduce her carbon footprint.